SIR GEOFFREY CROWTHER

Balances and Imbalances of Payments

The George H. Leatherbee Lectures
1957

GEOFFREY CROWTHER
Managing Director, The Economist

HARVARD UNIVERSITY
Graduate School of Business Administration
BOSTON, 1957

Library of Congress Catalog Card Number 57–11369

PRINTED AT
THE PLIMPTON PRESS
NORWOOD, MASS., U.S.A.

THE GEORGE H. LEATHERBEE LECTURES have been made possible by a grant to Harvard University in the will of Mr. Leatherbee, Harvard alumnus and Boston businessman.

A native of Massachusetts, Mr. Leatherbee was an active member of the Harvard Class of 1882. After graduation, he was engaged in the lumber business in Boston, in West Virginia, in Chicago, and again in Boston where he was treasurer of the Trimount Lumber Company at the time of his death in 1911. He bequeathed to Harvard a sum of money to be accumulated until the principal could support a lectureship, to be known as the "George H. Leatherbee Lectures," on some topic of current interest in commercial business or finance. It was his wish that the lectures be open to the public, as well as to members of the University.

Initiated in 1920, the lectures have covered such topics as Foreign Exchange, Income Taxation, Latin-American Trade, Problems of Inflation, and Economic Trends. Previous Leatherbee lecturers include O. M. W. Sprague, Wallace B. Donham, Sumner Slichter, Malcolm P. McNair, W. G. Cunningham, and Neil H. Borden.

The present volume is the second of the series to be published. *Administration and Blind Spots* by Wallace B. Donham was published by the Graduate School of Business Administration in 1952.

[iii]

Foreword

Sir Geoffrey Crowther at the time of delivering these lectures in April, 1957, was the Managing Director of *The Economist* magazine of London, a Director of the *Encyclopædia Brittanica* and of a number of other corporations. He was also a member of the governing bodies of five schools and colleges in Great Britain, a member of the committee of award of the Commonwealth Fund Fellowships, and Chairman of the Central Advisory Council for Education, advising the Minister of Education. His Knighthood, which we recognize in this foreword, was announced in the Queen's Birthday Honors List in June, while this book was in preparation.

From 1938 until 1956 Sir Geoffrey served as the Editor of *The Economist*. Already a distinguished magazine, it achieved new distinction during his editorship for the breadth of its coverage, the depth of its analysis, and the superb style of its presentation. It is indeed a journal of international importance.

Born at Leeds, he was educated in England, graduating from Clare College, Cambridge. He continued his studies in the United States, principally in Economics, at Yale University and at Columbia University from 1929 until 1931, a period in which he was the holder of one of the early Commonwealth Fund Fellowships. At that time he formed the interest in balance of payments problems which still continues, and which has resulted in the presently published lectures. Other studies in the same area of interest include "An Outline of Money" (1940) and "The Economic Reconstruction of Europe" (1948).

Modern means of transportation are shrinking the world to the point where an economic crisis in France, a crop failure in the Argentine, a political upset in Indonesia, take new importance to us because they are happenings to neighbors. In these lectures, Sir Geoffrey discusses problems less susceptible of ready solution than the technical obstacles to speedy transportation — the barriers to economic interchange which are created by distortions in balances of payments. His analysis indicates that many of the problems created by two wars and the great depression are finding their way to solution, but that one problem, often referred to as "the dollar shortage," will remain with us for a long time. Other experts may disagree (indeed some did at the lectures) but all will find Sir Geoffrey's ideas stimulating and presented with his usual clarity of style.

STANLEY F. TEELE
Dean

Soldiers Field
Boston, Massachusetts
June, 1957

Contents

I

The Nations' Pattern of Growth

THE HONOR of being invited to lecture under this Foundation and in this famous institution is one which I greatly prize. You who are members of the Business School are in the best position to form an accurate assessment of how high its standing is in the academic and business worlds of America. I could say nothing on that theme that would not be familiar to you. But I have often wondered whether you realise how powerful a lodestone the Harvard Business School is for the intelligent and ambitious youth of the whole of the free world. It has been my job for several years past to sift the applications of large numbers of young men who apply for scholarships and fellowships to continue their studies in the United States. Of those whose interests are economic, industrial, commercial or administrative — of those, in short, who want to make their careers in business — the overwhelming majority want to come here and would be bitterly disappointed to be sent elsewhere. In its own particular field — which is a wide one and an important one — the Harvard Graduate School of Business Administration has made itself the unchallenged leader of the world.

So intimidating is this pre-eminence, so awesome the serried authority of your Faculty, that it would have been presumptuous of me to have chosen a subject for these

[1]

lectures that was located on any of the main highways of your curriculum — presumptuous and foolhardy, for my downfall and exposure would have followed inevitably and rapidly. I have therefore chosen a subject that lies, not, indeed, I hope, outside the territory of your interests, but on one of the less frequented byways. It is a subject on which I did a certain amount of work long ago, in the days when I could still lay some claim to be an economist and before journalism, with its kaleidoscopic superficialities, had entirely eroded my academic standing. I am grateful to you for giving me an opportunity to bring this work up to date and to use it as a base for surveying some of the practical problems that plague the administrator in the present day.

My subject turns on and around the estimates that are made periodically by every self-respecting country of its balance of international payments. It is worth pausing to reflect how much of modern economics has come to be based on two statistical exercises, on the estimates of national income and on the estimates of the balance of payments. I like to think that I am not yet a very old man; and yet in my student days, neither the balance of payments nor the national income was known to us, save as an abstract conception, to which none but a few inaccurate amateurs had attempted to give quantitative substance. When, in those days, we discussed domestic economic phenomena, it was in terms of their effect upon prices or (if we were very up to date) on the level of employment; we would hardly have known what was meant by their effect on the national income. Similarly, international economics turned on movements of gold, their causes and effects, and the balance of payments was an academic exercise. Yet to-day, only a generation later,

governments employ whole batteries of skilled statisticians to make the most complete, frequent and authorita-
tive estimates of these two elements, and very nearly the
whole of economic discussion revolves round one or the
other or both.   One of the enterprises that I am storing
up for my retirement is to apply the technique of the
comic strip to the teaching of economics, and my two
chief characters will, infallibly, be christened Nat and
Bal.   There is a question in my mind whether I should
represent them as villains or as heroes.   How happy was
the world that knew them not!   Have they simply appeared to measure our misery?   Or could it be that they
have caused the trouble — you never know with statistics,
or with statisticians?   I have often wondered this about
unemployment statistics — there never seemed to be
nearly so much unemployment until somebody set out
to measure it.   And who ever heard of a balance-of-payments crisis before there were any balance-of-payments
estimates?

But I am not only digressing, I am digressing into lev-
ity, and I must remember where I am.   I am addressing
an audience of businessmen, *pre-, ex-* or *proto-*.   And perhaps to such an audience the first point to make about the
balance of payments is that it is not strictly analogous to
either of the great statistical formularies with which businessmen are familiar — it is neither a balance sheet nor a
revenue-and-expenditure account.   It is much more in
the nature of a cash account or day ledger.   It is a record
of all the transactions that have taken place between the
country concerned and the rest of the world, a list of all
the payments, inwards and outwards, whether capital or
current.   There is no particular reason why the area for
which the estimate is made should be that of a nation.   I

have often wondered, in driving through a small town, either here or in England, how it balanced its books over a year, what the in-payments and the out-payments were — in short, what its balance of payments was — and I remember a very gallant and interesting attempt in *Fortune* magazine a good many years ago to do just that for a small town in the Middle West, which was, I believe, chiefly the work of an eminent Harvard professor. In practice, however, balances of payments are regularly compiled only for nations. They have been collected together, before the war in an annual series of reports published by the League of Nations, since the war in a new series issued by the International Monetary Fund. All the figures in these lectures are taken from these two sources, to which I pay my grateful tribute.

There is one respect in which the balance of payments does resemble a corporation balance sheet or an income and expenditure account. Like all the rest of the progeny of the great invention of double-entry bookkeeping, it has to balance. The totals of the two sides have to come out equal and, as with other forms of accounts, if the figures don't naturally come out that way, you have to cook them until they do. I remember a lady of my acquaintance telling me how much she had suffered in her youth from her father's insistence on accurately balanced accounts, until she discovered that he could be satisfied with a large final item frankly labelled "shy." Most countries' balances of payments include items like that, not always so candidly disclosed. The opposite also sometimes occurs — not only are entries that cannot be identified put in, but some that can be identified are taken out. I quote from the official publication, "The Balance of International Payments of the United States in 1928":

[4]

The surveys for 1924, 1925 and 1926 contained estimates of the sums paid to foreigners for smuggled liquor. . . . certain public officers found ground to object to such publicity.

Well do I remember the vehement form that these objections by "certain public officers" took, but my memory does not extend to whether they held that these undoubted payments should simply be omitted, or that they should be added to the item of "missionary and charitable contributions, etc." Perhaps I have said enough to indicate that no balance of payments, however carefully compiled, can be more than an approximate estimate of what it purports to measure.

Many of the national estimates are most complicated documents, presenting their figures under scores of distinct headings. This is particularly true of the estimates made by the United States Department of Commerce, which are models of their kind. But for the purposes of the broad analysis with which I am concerned this afternoon, we can confine ourselves to three comprehensive headings, Trade, Interest and Capital. Let me spend a few minutes defining them.

Trade, of course, includes not only all forms of buying and selling of goods, but also the whole range of current services, such as payments or receipts for shipping and railroad freights, insurance premiums, banking commissions, patent royalties, motion picture and book royalties, governmental expenditures (such as the pay of troops overseas) and — most important — tourist receipts or payments. In short, Trade is to be taken as including all forms of commerce, visible and invisible.

Some people also include under Services, and there-

[5]

fore in Trade, a country's receipts or payments of interest and dividends on capital lent or borrowed. It seems to me preferable, however, not to do this. To call interest received an "invisible export" seems to me a distortion of language, since nothing at all, visible or invisible, is currently exported. I therefore reckon these payments, received or made, as a separate major item.

These first two items, Trade and Interest, taken together, constitute the Balance of Current Transactions, which measures the extent to which, in the year in question, the country is or is not paying its way. And since the whole account must balance, it follows that the third item, Capital Movements, must be equal in magnitude and opposite in sign to the total of the first two. If a country has received, in respect of all its current transactions, Trade and Interest together, more than it has paid out — if, in the familiar language, it has a favourable or positive balance of current transactions — then it must inevitably have increased its external capital assets — that is, it must have exported capital — to precisely the same net amount. If it has not done so by formal and deliberate loans, then it must either have imported gold (and paid out money for it) or increased its holdings or deposits in foreign banks. This third item of Capital is, therefore, an amalgam of all kinds of movements of funds on capital account. For convenience, governmental donations, such as United States foreign aid, are usually entered here.

There are some further definitions which are necessary for the analysis. It is necessary to define Creditors and Debtors on the one hand, and Lenders and Borrowers on the other. The distinction ought, I think, to be reasonably clear. Creditor or Debtor refers to the pre-existing state of a nation's capital account, as brought forward from the past. A creditor country is one which, at the beginning of the year, had more external assets than liabilities, and owed less to other countries than they owed to it. A debtor country, in the same way, starts the year with a net liability. The test of creditor or debtor status, therefore, is whether a country, on balance, receives or pays interest and dividends. It is shown by a positive or a negative sign in the Interest column. (This, incidentally, is not always or strictly true. It is possible for a country which is a net debtor on capital account nevertheless to be a net receiver of interest. This has been true of Britain in several post-war years and is to be explained by the fact that Britain's external assets are nowadays mainly high yielding industrial investments, while its liabilities are short-term banking debts with low rates of interest. But this is an exceptional case, and for practical purposes we can safely assume that a creditor is a net receiver of interest and a debtor a net payer.)

So much for Creditor and Debtor. The other pair of terms, Lender and Borrower, refer, not to the present state of the Interest item, but to the present state of the Capital item, to whether, in the year in question, the country is exporting or importing capital. Lending and Borrowing are not comprehensive descriptions, for the repayment of past borrowings has the same effect as present lending — both are exports of capital. Similarly, a country which is, on balance, accepting repayment of its past lendings, and living on the proceeds, is importing capital, just as if it was borrowing. Thus Lending must be taken to include Repaying and Borrowing to include Drawing on Assets.

It is at this point, I think, that I must relieve the tedium of the proceedings by quoting poetry. You will remember the seven ages of Man —

                              At first the infant,
Mewling and puking in the nurse's arms.
And then the whining schoolboy, with his satchel,
And shining morning face, creeping like snail
Unwillingly to school. And then the lover,
Sighing like furnace, with a woful ballad
Made to his mistress' eyebrow. Then a soldier,
Full of strange oaths, and bearded like the pard,
Jealous in honour, sudden and quick in quarrel,
Seeking the bubble reputation
Even in the cannon's mouth. And then the justice,
In fair round belly with good capon lin'd,
With eyes severe, and beard of formal cut,
Full of wise saws and modern instances;
And so he plays his part. The sixth age shifts
Into the lean and slipper'd pantaloon,
With spectacles on nose and pouch on side,
His youthful hose well sav'd a world too wide
For his shrunk shank; and his big manly voice,
Turning again towards childish treble, pipes
And whistles in his sound. Last score of all,
That ends this strange eventful history,
Is second childishness, and mere oblivion,
Sans teeth, sans eyes, sans taste, sans everything.

I have no ambition to compete with Shakespeare. I shall not essay blank verse, and I can compass only six stages. But I think it is possible to match this standard progression of a man's estate with a similar progression in a nation's development. I would now draw your attention to Table 1. (See page 64.) This sets out in sym-

[8]

bols the six stages which I am going to describe. First of all, however, let me point out that, in every column, a plus sign means an inward payment, or receipt, a minus sign means an outward payment. This is obvious, I think, in the first two columns, where a plus means a sale of goods or services, and a minus a purchase. A little more care is perhaps needed in the third column, where a minus means lending and a plus borrowing. The clue to remember is that the symbols always refer to the money; when you lend the money goes away from you, and a minus sign is the appropriate one. Two pluses, or two minuses, in one column, mean a relatively large in-payment or out-payment.

Let us start by imagining a virgin, undeveloped territory, wholly innocent of any capital and earning its existence by scratching the soil with hand tools or hunting wild beasts, and neither importing nor exporting anything — such a country, let us say, as the North American continent was when the Pilgrim Fathers landed. Now when such a country is first drawn into the world economy, it starts by importing both goods and capital. External capital provides the funds for opening it up, and sends in the rails and the locomotives, the bridging material and the mining equipment, the ploughs and the looms that are needed. Year by year, such a country's imports of goods are far greater than its exports; it pays the interest on one year's borrowings out of the next year's borrowings. To this country I have given the description of Immature Debtor-Borrower and you will find it represented on the first line of the table. It is a debtor because it pays interest; it is a borrower because it is still importing capital; and it is immature because even its balance of trade is negative.

[9]

In due course of time, however, the capital investment matures. The railroads have been built, the prairies ploughed and sown, the forests cut and sawn, and the goods begin to move out. A time comes when exports begin to exceed imports and a plus sign appears in the first column. At first, however, the net balance of exports is not enough to cover the whole of the interest that has to be paid on the accumulated borrowings of the early years; some continuing further borrowing is therefore necessary, though presently on a declining scale. The country is therefore still a debtor and still a borrower. But it can now be called a Mature Debtor-Borrower. The United States reached this stage in the year 1873 and stayed in it right up to the first World War in 1914, a net exporter of goods, but still borrowing every year, for further development, part of what she paid in interest.

As the development progresses and the export trade builds up, a day comes when the export surplus exceeds the outgoings on interest. The country can then put an end to its borrowings. It has, for the first time, a favourable balance of current transactions and can start exporting capital. It has finished its apprenticeship and can now prepare to bear its burdens. This, presumably, is the lover, making his woful ballad to his mistress' eyebrow. If the export of capital takes the form of repaying the development loans of the early years, then a country in this stage is best described as a Debtor-Repayer. Often, however, the original development took the form, not of governmental loans with redemption dates, but of direct investments by foreign capitalists, who will not wish to withdraw their capital when it matures. In these cases, therefore, the young country's export of capital takes the form of lending to other countries, perhaps at an earlier stage of development than itself, and it is best described as a Debtor-Lender. In either case, however, the symbols will be as they are shown on the third line, an export surplus of trade, a net payment of interest and, because the positive figure in the first column has become larger than the negative figure in the second column, a net export of capital in the third column.

Time passes again, and our developing country, having passed from Borrower to Repayer or Lender, now also passes from Debtor to Creditor — that is to say, its steady export of capital reaches the point at which its external assets exceed its external liabilities and the tide of interest turns inwards. This is the fourth stage, when a country is beginning to feel its strength in the world and to throw its weight about. It is the stage of the soldier, full of strange oaths, sudden and quick in quarrel. So we will call it the Immature Creditor-Lender — a creditor because it receives interest, a lender because it exports capital, but immature because it still sells more, in goods and services, than it buys.

As a nation piles up capital assets, and as its interest receipts increase, a time comes when its debtors insist that, if they are to pay at all, they must pay in goods. Or, to put the same point in another way, a time comes when a rich country decides to consume some of its interest receipts and not to re-invest them all every year; the only way it can do that is by importing more goods than it sells, or by taking longer and more expensive vacations abroad. In short, the net balance of trade turns negative, and the stage of the Mature Creditor-Lender is reached. This is the position that Great Britain enjoyed all through the golden years of the capitalist era, from the 1850s until the first World War and beyond. This was

the period when Britain laid down the law to the world
— the justice, full of wise saws and modern instances.

There is still a sixth stage. The Mature Creditor-
Lender, the fifth stage we have just been dealing with,
consumes part of its interest receipts and lends the rest.
The sixth stage arrives when the process goes further,
when a nation consumes not only all its interest receipts
but more besides, and therefore has to borrow — or, more
likely, draw on its capital assets — to balance the books.
In other words, the negative balance of trade becomes
larger than the net interest receipts. This is the stage of
the Creditor-Borrower or Creditor-Consumer-of-Capital.
It is the stage that a man reaches after he has retired from
active life, when he lives partly on the interest from his
past investments, partly by consuming his capital.
Clearly, it is the stage of the slippered pantaloon.

I said at the start that there were only six stages. And
so there are, in the sense that the signs cannot be arranged
in a seventh pattern, bearing in mind that the third must
be opposite to the sum of the first two, so that plus-plus-
plus and minus-minus-minus are both impossible. But it
can happen, as I shall demonstrate in a moment, that a
mature and developed country can become so improvi-
dent, or be so overwhelmed by the calamities of war, that
it can fall right back to the start again and become a
Debtor-Borrower. So this is the seventh stage after all,
the second childishness, and a country which does not
quickly take steps to get out of it will soon find itself sans
teeth, sans eyes, sans taste, sans everything.

You will appreciate, of course, that my account of the
rise of a country from early economic beginnings to full
maturity is purely schematic. I cannot produce any annual series of figures proving that any country has gone

regularly right through the gamut. From what we know of the economic history of the United States it seems to me probable that this country did in fact go the whole course. Certainly, it must have started as a Debtor-Borrower, and remained so until the republic was nearly a hundred years old. From the 1870s onwards, however, the total of interest payable began to exceed each year's new borrowings, while the enormous development of the country produced the export surplus that enabled the interest to be paid. This Mature Debtor-Borrower status lasted about forty years, right up to the outbreak of war in 1914. The gigantic cataclysm of the first World War enabled America to run through the next two stages in a few years. The large exports of war materials enabled her not only to redeem all her outstanding debts but even to become a net lender. Not only so, but her interest income rapidly became so large that she was able, in some years at least, to import more goods and services than she exported and to become a Mature Creditor-Lender.

Other countries, however, start halfway. Britain, for example, never borrowed until the two world wars (except, of course, in the sense in which a banker "borrows" from his customers). And Canada has never ceased to be a Debtor-Borrower — not, indeed, through any lack of instability or progressiveness in her economic arrangements, but because the unparalleled magnitude of her natural resources, coupled with the existence just south of the border of an enormous pool of capital, has never ceased to attract a large flow of investment from external sources. As usually happens, reality fits only awkwardly into the theoretical pattern.

It is time for me to ask you to turn to the other tables that are in your hands. These show the actual figures of the balances of payments of a number of countries at three different periods of recent history. You will see that in each table there are six columns of figures. The first, second and last columns are the familiar three of Table 1. The third column is simply an aggregation of columns 1 and 2. The fourth and fifth columns are, contrariwise, a breakdown of column 6, showing how much of the capital movement was in the form of gold and how much in a change of the various forms of international indebtedness. Columns 3 and 6 are, of course, equal and opposite to each other. Perhaps I ought also to say a word of caution about the gold column. The plus and minus signs relate to the way the money moves, not the gold. A plus sign in this column therefore means an export, or loss, of gold, just as a plus sign in column one means an export of some other form of goods.

Let us turn first to Table 2 for the year 1937. (See page 65.) I chose this as the most stable year of the 1930s, after the storms of the Great Depression had largely blown themselves out and before the last feverish and nervous preparations for the impending war began. In so far as there was a pre-war normality, this is it. The table is somewhat affected by the fact that, for one reason or another, only sixteen countries can be included. But they include most of the financially important ones except Switzerland. Germany, being cooped up behind Dr. Schacht's exchange controls, hardly played a significant role at that time. I think the picture the table paints is broadly correct in spite of the omissions.

The most interesting thing about it, to my mind, is the way the nations are bunched in the middle. Very little lending or borrowing was going on. As it happens, the three borrowers shown in Class B all stood in a favoured

[14]

relationship to one of the world's great capital markets, South Africa and Australia to London, Poland to Paris. It is true that the United States appears, formally, as a lender. But you will observe that America in fact imported gold to twice the amount of its net capital balance, so that the flow of all kinds of capital other than gold was inwards. Moreover, unlike many other years of the interval between the wars, in this year the United States sold more goods and services than it bought. The other two great capital-exporting countries, France and Britain, had slipped into the Creditor-Borrower classification — that is to say, they were lending less fresh money abroad than they were receiving in repayment of past loans.

The picture, in short, is one of an international financial system in stagnation. The post-war gold standard, so painfully rebuilt in the 1920s, had broken down in the early thirties. In those depression years there were wild movements of funds, but by 1937 everything had settled down to a minimum of movements of any kind. London and Paris were still making small loans to their favoured clients, but on the whole were more concerned to gather in repayments. American investors' fingers had been so badly burned by the foreign loans of the late 1920s that they were not interested in making any more. Indeed, capital was flowing into the United States for safe-keeping, and America's books were balanced only by massive imports of gold.

This was the pre-war picture. I want you now to turn to Table 3 (see pages 66–67), which shows the picture in the years 1949 to 1951 — that is, roughly the years of the Marshall Plan, complicated at the end by the Korean war and the commodity boom it caused. This time 33 nations are shown, including all those that are of any importance except, again, Switzerland, which did not begin to make estimates until later than this period.

The most striking contrast with 1937 is, of course, the long list of Debtor-Borrowers. Since Marshall aid is treated in these tables as a movement of capital, its beneficiaries naturally appear as Borrowers. What is surprising is that so many of them are Debtor-Borrowers, in the immature class, and for such large amounts too. Take, for example, the case of France at the top of the list, borrowing on the average of these three years over $650 million a year. Granted all the suffering and dislocation that France suffered during the war, was there not something very unsound in the position revealed? What also were the big commercial nations of South America, Argentina and Brazil, doing in the list of Immature Debtor-Borrowers? Surely they were wrong, at their time of life, to be importing more than they were exporting? At the other end of the table, there is a shortage of lenders, other than the gigantic figure for the United States. ("Immaturity" as a Creditor-Lender, of course, is a misnomer in this year; the large export surplus simply reflects the goods that were shipped abroad under the Marshall Plan. Even so, it does not include any military goods.)

In short, this is a picture of a world grappling with an emergency. Note, for example, how small are the figures in the Gold column. Clearly, any form of gold standard had ceased to function; a credit system of some sort was being held together only by massive injections of free American dollars. Even so, there are one or two signs of stability and normal progress. Australia and New Zealand, for example, riding the wool boom, are among the Repayers, as are Pakistan and Finland. Notice too

[16]

the appearance of the oil states, Iran, Iraq and Venezuela, with their enormous payments of interest very nearly borne by their no less enormous exports of oil. The United Kingdom, too, has crept back to its natural place as a Mature Creditor-Lender — though in these particular years its receipts of aid appear to have exceeded its loans to other countries, chiefly in the Commonwealth, so that there was a net gain of gold. And, finally, Canada appears as a Mature Debtor-Borrower, or one might more properly say, as a Perpetual Borrower-Developer, constantly borrowing more for further development.

Finally, we turn to Table 4 (see pages 68–69), which gives the figures for the latest triennial period for which they have all yet been collected. Let me draw your attention first to the figures for the United States, at the bottom. You will see that the figure for American foreign lending (which you will remember includes non-military aid payments), though still large, is very much smaller than it was. Indeed, it is slightly smaller than the mounting total of American interest and dividend receipts, pushing the United States into the Mature classification. Notice also the United Kingdom in the Immature classification, which is again a misnomer, as it results from the tremendous efforts made by British industry in these years to build up the export trade. Western Germany, its currency reformed, has bounded in three years from Class A to Class C, from the second largest import of capital in 1949–51 to the second largest export in 1952–54. At the bottom end, the creditors' end, of the table one can say that in these years affairs were returning to normal. The supplies of international capital were reasonably large, and they were coming from the right quarters. Note in particular that two of the oil countries, Iraq

[17]

and Venezuela, had crossed the line and become Repayers; Iran would have joined them if these had not happened to be the years of Dr. Mossadegh.

But at the top end of the table, the borrowers' end, there is still sad evidence of things being awry. Look who is still absorbing the supply of international capital, which should be going into development. European countries are still four of the first six. Can it really be believed that these massive injections of capital into France and Italy, Turkey and Yugoslavia, were being fruitfully used to build up export industries, the only way in which these countries can hope to balance their books, let alone start any repayment that may be due? Australia and New Zealand, the wool boom broken, had slipped back into Class A. Were their borrowings being used for further development, which would eventually pay its way in the coin of exports, or simply to sustain the consuming standards, and importing standards, to which their city populations had grown accustomed? What are Norway, and to a minor extent Denmark, doing as Immature Debtor-Borrowers, when the Netherlands, whose economy is in many ways similar and which suffered more damage during the war, is so large a Creditor-Lender? It looks as if, in these years, far too much of the world's available capital was being used to sustain political policies rather than economic development.

I have tried in these tables to present an overall picture of the world economy as it was developed in the postwar years. The defect of an overall picture, however, is that it has to ignore so many of the qualifications and obscure so many of the difficulties. In my second lecture, therefore, I am going to take up for discussion the largest of these hidden snags. All of the figures I have been presenting today have been converted into United States dollars. As a statistical exercise, that is permissible. But in actual commerce in the world of today, the biggest difficulty is precisely that currencies cannot be converted into dollars. It is to this thorny subject that I shall turn in the second lecture.

II

One World? Or Two? Or Twenty?

IN MY FIRST LECTURE, I tried to sketch out what might be
called the ideal pattern of development among the nations. I drew a picture of a country starting from the
virgin soil and beginning to borrow from others the
means of its own development. To begin with, interest
on the first borrowings has to be met out of further borrowings, as is usual with all gradual development projects.
But gradually the development matures, the wheat pours
out of the prairies, an export surplus is built up and the
borrowed capital starts to be repaid. So a country can be
imagined to move from immaturity to maturity as a
Debtor-Borrower, to the halfway stage of a Debtor-Repayer and then to Creditor-Lender status.

This progression is not entirely imaginary. As I sug-
gested in the first lecture, the United States itself has
passed through all these stages, and though we have not
exact figures for every year, we can date pretty closely the
transitions from one stage to another. But when, towards
the end of my first lecture, I laid before you the figures for
the various countries of the world in three recent periods,
one just before the second World War and two after, it
was immediately apparent that the regularity of the world
in which the United States grew up has disappeared, and
that there is very little correspondence between the posi-
tions that the countries occupy in the tables and the stage

of development which, from general knowledge of their condition, one would have expected them to have reached. Even so, however, there is a whole set of distortions of the ideal pattern which a table constructed in the manner of those which accompanied my first lecture does not reveal. It is to these latter-day complications, arising out of the fact that currencies are no longer freely convertible into each other, that I now turn.

You will recall that, in the text books, money is said to have three functions to perform — as a unit of account, as a medium of exchange and as a store of value. Now in saying of the tables that accompanied my first lecture that all the figures had been "converted into United States dollars," I was, strictly speaking, using the dollar only as a unit of account, as a convenient common measure to which all the national units of account could be reduced, in order to make comparison between them possible. But there was a clear implication in the adding up that the dollar could also be used as a medium of exchange — or at least that there was something, of fixed value in terms of the dollar, that could be so used. When one shows a country running a deficit in its merchandise trade, and covering that deficit, partly by net earnings on account of services (invisible trade, as it is sometimes called), partly by receipts of interest on foreign assets, and having enough left over to make some new loans, one is tacitly assuming that these various sums are in fact available to be set against each other.

For nearly two decades now, this assumption has not in fact been valid. It takes a bit of an effort to remember how recent this change is. Right up to the Great Depression — say to the year 1931, only a quarter of a century ago — it was universally assumed, and almost universally

[21]

true, that all currencies were freely convertible into all other currencies — that is to say, that any trader or investor who became possessed of any of the world's currencies could take it to his bank and have it converted into any other currency that he chose to specify. The rate at which the exchange was accomplished might indeed vary, and frequently did so. But that the exchange could be accomplished at *some* rate was taken for granted. The first systematic breach in this assumption — except for temporary ones by minor countries on the verge of bankruptcy — was made by some of the Central European countries in the years from 1932 onwards. The ringleader was Nazi Germany, so again the impression was given that the blocking of a currency was a dictator's trick, to be classified with secret police and the execution of opposition leaders. In the free democratic world, in spite of the serious difficulties with which many countries were faced in the depression years, it remained true that money in one place could be converted, for any purpose, into money at another place.

Since 1939, that has ceased to be true over by far the greater part of the world. I sometimes wonder if the inhabitants of the United States realize in what exceptional conditions they live. You, in deciding where you shall travel and from whom you shall buy, need give no thought to the means of payment; your dollars will be accepted in exchange for any currency in the world. But in that you are quite unique. There are other countries where the restrictions are in practice so light that they are barely noticeable — Switzerland for example. There is a whole range, in the world, of degrees of freedom to convert. But almost everywhere there is the legal apparatus of control. It cannot any longer be taken for granted that a holding of one currency can be converted into another, or if it can be converted for one purpose that it can be converted for another. Perhaps I should also explain, before I pass on, that even the word "convertibility," as it is used in public discussion, has come to have a meaning far more restricted than the pre-war world would have recognized. Convertibility of the pound sterling was promised in the American-British Loan Agreement of 1945, was attempted and failed in 1947, and has been talked about ever since. But this meant only that foreign, non-British holders of sterling should have the right to convert it into other currencies, not the British people themselves — and, moreover, foreign holders only if they had acquired their sterling through current trade, not by capital transactions. To such a pass has the financial world been reduced, that this miserably restricted licence masquerades in the costume of freedom.

Obviously, such widespread restrictions upon the convertibility of currencies introduce severe complications into the nations' balances of payments. The classical case is that of Canada. The Canadian economy had grown up on a triangular pattern. The main market for Canadian exports was in Great Britain. It was there that the wheat, the timber, the fruit and much of the paper were sold. But the great source of Canada's imports was the United States. The triangle was completed by an act of conversion. Canada earned pounds sterling and spent U.S. dollars, and so long as pounds could be freely converted into U.S. dollars, there was no occasion for anyone to worry. Indeed, there was a capital triangle superimposed on the trade triangle. The traditional source of capital for Canadian development, certainly until the first World War,

[23]

and in large measure right up to the second World War, was the City of London. But the money thus raised was often largely spent in the United States — that is to say, the actual materials for development came from south of the border. Again, the process entirely depended upon the fact that pounds borrowed in London could be converted into dollars to be spent in Pittsburgh and Detroit.

With the outbreak of war in 1939 the essential third side of the triangle was broken, and after the war it was not restored. It took a little time for the Canadians to lose their feeling that, in refusing convertibility, the British Government was simply being stupid or perverse — indeed, I don't know that that feeling has even yet entirely vanished. But the plain fact, at least as seen from London, was that U.S. dollars could not be made available for the conversion of Canada's sterling earnings because Britain simply did not have the dollars, and could not get them by the conversion of its own earnings in foreign countries. As a result, far-reaching and most painful adjustments have been imposed on Canada's trading pattern. She has had to find new markets for her goods and, at times, to watch very closely her imports from the United States. The process has been carried out with matchless skill — I have often thought that the small body of government servants at Ottawa is without an equal for competence in the world — but it has also been assisted by the fortunate circumstance that Canada has been able, year by year, to attract massive imports of American capital for the development of her great natural resources. Without the oil and the aluminum and the uranium and the iron ore, Canada might have been crippled by the sudden withdrawal of the assumption that all currencies are convertible into each other.

[24]

Canada is perhaps the leading case of a country which has had to re-orient the direction of a substantial part of its trade. That was because, firstly, the destination of Canada's exports was unduly sharply distinguished from the source of her imports, and, secondly, because this vital third side of the triangle happened to join two currencies where the breakdown of convertibility was severe. Not many countries were as hard hit. But nearly all of them would be crippled in their trade if earnings in one country could not be used for payments in another. As an exhibit, I draw your attention to the table, Table 5 (see page 70), which shows the balances of the United States' transactions in a specimen year with several different groups of countries. You will notice the variation in the last line between pluses and minuses. If there were no convertibility of currencies, every one of these columns would have to be made to come out at exactly zero, and much the most probable way of accomplishing this would be by cutting down some of the trading items at the top or by defaulting on the interest item lower down. Moreover, this would have to be done, not for each group of nations as shown in the table, but for each national currency individually.

Fortunately, however, the process of dividing the world up into separate currency compartments has not gone quite as far as at one time seemed probable. Immediately after the war, much of the world's trade was reduced to a pure barter basis — country A would buy from country B only to the exact amount that country B would simultaneously buy from country A. Had this continued, the world would have lost most of the benefits of the division of labour and would have been greatly impoverished thereby. But as things settled down, various spheres of

[25]

wider convertibility appeared. I said a minute or two ago that there are very few countries in the world today where, as in the United States, you can convert your money into any currency you choose. But in almost every country on this side of the Iron Curtain you can convert your money, at least for the purposes of current trade, into a great many foreign currencies, though not into all. Let me briefly list the main areas of convertibility that exist in the world today.

First there are those currencies which are, for all practical purposes, wholly free and convertible. The United States dollar is at the head of the list, followed by the Canadian dollar, the Swiss franc and one or two others. If you have any of these currencies you can still, broadly speaking, do what you will with it. The difficulty is that, for most of the peoples of the world, these are precisely the currencies that are hardest to obtain — which is, of course, not at all a coincidence.

Secondly there is the Sterling Area. This has been much misunderstood, not least perhaps in the United States, where for a long time after the war it seemed to be regarded, even in Washington and by people who should have known better, as a sort of extension into the monetary sphere of outdated and wicked British imperialism, a means by which the imperialists in London could, by some mysterious means, levy hidden tribute on their helpless victims. It is perhaps enough of an answer to this to point out that the Republic of Ireland, as fierce an opponent of British Imperialism as there is to be found even in the city of Boston, is and always has been a member of the Sterling Area. In fact, the Area is not co-terminous with the British Commonwealth of Nations. There are members of the Commonwealth — Canada for instance

— which are not members of the Area, and there are non-British members of the Area, such as Iraq, Burma, Ireland and Iceland. It is, in fact, an arrangement of mutual convenience among its members, who agree to pool their reserves of gold and dollars under a single central management and to settle their mutual transactions by entries on the books of the Bank of England. Within the whole of the Sterling Area, with one or two minor exceptions, payments for any purpose are free of control. If a resident of the Bahamas wants to remit money to New Zealand for any purpose, he simply writes a check and mails it, just as if it were a transaction between Maine and California. The Sterling Area, in fact, is by far the largest area of virtually complete convertibility in the world, from which the whole world draws benefit. If an Italian company sells chocolates to Malta, it can use the proceeds to import cocoa beans from Ghana. What is perhaps more important to American manufacturing corporations, if you have a branch factory anywhere in the Sterling Area, you can sell your product everywhere in the Sterling Area free, not indeed from customs duties, but from any difficulty of payment or from any prohibition on financial grounds. This is an aspect of the matter to which I shall recur.

Thirdly, there has been built up in recent years, with great ingenuity, an area of partial convertibility in Europe known as the European Payments Union, or E.P.U. The convertibility that this provides is not nearly as far reaching as that which prevails in the Sterling Area. The members of E.P.U. do not undertake, as the members of the Sterling Area do, to settle all their mutual transactions by book entries at a central bank. There is a most complicated system by which the mutual indebtednesses

[27]

are worked out every month and, if they are over a certain figure, are settled partly in gold. And because of this, the members do not permit convertibility for all transactions. If I, a resident of England, want to buy a house in New Zealand, or to spend six months in Jamaica, I can do so by writing a check. But if I want to make a capital purchase in France, I must seek permission, which is as likely as not to be withheld, and my vacation at Monte Carlo will be limited to the time that I can exist there on one hundred pounds, increased or diminished by exposure to the main industry of the principality. Nevertheless, though most members of E.P.U. do not permit convertibility for capital transactions or for some kinds of services, there is virtually complete convertibility for merchandise trade and for transport charges, insurance and the like. Broadly speaking, although the E.P.U. does not solve the payments problem for the European *governments* — they still have their monthly clearing to meet — it does remove the payments problem, for all practical purposes, from the European *businessman,* who is enabled to go ahead and do his business without having to worry about whether he will be allowed to pay or be paid. Indeed, this mechanism for clearing the many-cornered trade of the European nations has worked so well that it has been possible to proceed to far-reaching schemes for reducing tariffs and dismantling quantitative restrictions, to such a point that, as you know, active negotiations are now proceeding for a virtual customs union among six of the Western European nations and for a Free Trade Area between these six and another six countries. There is one further point about the E.P.U. and the Sterling Area that is worth making. The United Kingdom is a member of both. This means that the benefits of the E.P.U., within

[28]

its limits, are extended to trade between Europe and the whole of the Sterling Area. When Germany sells machinery to Burma, the proceeds can be used to pay for wool from Australia or tobacco from Rhodesia.

There are other, smaller, pools of convertibility that I have not mentioned. Thus there is a franc area between France and parts of the French Union and an escudo area that embraces Portugal and its overseas territories. There are also a number of special arrangements. For example, an arrangement known as the Hague Club has recently been made between Brazil and some of the countries of Western Europe whereby the cruzeiro, hitherto one of the most tightly restricted currencies of the world, is made partly convertible among the members of the club, and the proceeds of sales of coffee in Holland are made available for the payment of interest on debt to Britain or for the purchase of machinery from Germany.

One could go on almost indefinitely elaborating the details of the world's present currency arrangements. But I think it is possible to collect them into a single generalisation. The Sterling Area and the European Payments Union, between them, comprise most of the trading nations of the free world in the continents of Europe, Asia, Africa and Australasia. This means that, so far as concerns current trade (not capital, that is far more complicated), substantial freedom of payments prevails in the whole of the Eastern Hemisphere outside the Iron Curtain. Also within the Dollar Area, which can be defined as extending as far south as the southern littoral of the Caribbean, but excluding the British, French and Dutch West Indies, there is substantial freedom from payments restrictions. But between these two great areas, between the Dollar Area and the Free Eastern Hemisphere, there is still tight control and restriction. If you are in business in one of these areas, then you can trade *within* that area with substantially no more interference from governments (and in some instances less) than before the war. But between these two great areas, there is restriction and control. If you are in business in the Eastern Hemisphere, you will be allowed — and indeed encouraged — to sell to the Dollar Area, but you will find it very difficult to buy. If you live and trade in the Dollar Area, you will find it easy to buy from the Eastern Hemisphere, but very difficult to sell.

Clearly, this state of affairs is a great deal better than the complete chaos and barter that at one time seemed probable. But equally clearly it falls a long way short of that One World which Wendell Willkie made his slogan and at which American policy aimed, in the economic sphere as in the political, in the years after the war. I would characterise the present position in this way. The ideal would be One World. The pit we nearly fell into was to have Two Score, or Three Score, Worlds. We have in fact finished up with Two Worlds.

This, of course, is a bit of an over-simplification. There is the whole of the Communist bloc, which really constitutes a third world, but it is for most purposes outside the ambit of the trading community. There is the whole of South America south of Venezuela, in which each country is a law unto itself — sometimes several laws at once. And there are occasional exceptions elsewhere, of which perhaps Spain and Japan are the chief. But all of these exceptions taken together would, I think, account for barely ten per cent of the world's commerce. Having duly noted their existence, I propose to forget about them and return to my broad, and broadly true, generalisation.

[30]

For all practical purposes, there is not One Financial and Commercial World, but Two Worlds, revolving respectively round the dollar and the pound sterling. Within each world there is substantial convertibility of currencies and freedom of payments. Between the two worlds, there is still a tight control and restriction — which would be tighter still if it were not for the generous flow of aid, and of other payments without material consideration, that still moves from the United States to the Eastern Hemisphere.

The existence of this division creates real problems, not only for governments, but also for every business administrator who is interested in developing an export business. Let us suppose, for example, that you are a manufacturer in the United States of a form of specialised machinery — let us say, machine tools. Your machines are not quite the only ones in the world that will do their job— there is a German machine in existence — but they are generally considered to be the most efficient. And if only you could get your volume up, you are confident that you could make them the cheapest of their kind in the world, in spite of the high American wages that you have to pay. I think you will agree that I have chosen a case that is not untypical. There is a considerable potential market for your machine tools in every industrialised country in the world. How can you best tap this market? Now clearly, if One World is some day coming back — if, that is, in a few years' time, you can expect to be able to ship to most countries, perhaps with a tariff duty to pay, but with no exchange control forbidding your customer to remit to you in the United States — clearly, if that is the prospect, you will be wise to concentrate all your production in your own plant in the Connecticut River valley, or in

[31]

Ohio, where you can get your volume up and your costs down. But if the outlook is that Two Worlds will continue, then this course of action is likely to cost you your market. There is a machine available in Germany, and every government that is a member of either the Sterling Area or of the European Payments Union will tell its industrialists that they must buy the German machine in preference to yours, unless it is very much more expensive or very much less efficient. In these circumstances, what you must do is to set up a subsidiary company and build a branch factory, either in Germany itself, or in England or in Scotland (American industries seem to have a remarkable preference for Scotland as a location for their branch factories — perhaps they labour under the delusion that certain Scotch products are cheaper in Scotland than in England), or you could put it in Belgium or Switzerland or elsewhere. It does not follow that you will have to do a complete job there, possibly the frame, the motor and the assembly, while you send the real heart of the machine over from here. All the advantages of quantity production may not be lost, depending on the bargain you can strike with the foreign government. But you will have to incur the greater part of your costs in some Eastern Hemisphere country, so that the so-called "dollar-content" of your machine is small, before you can hope to sell as freely as your German rival. But, in a Two-World system, you will only need one such branch factory, and from it you will be able to supply an enormous range of countries. (As I was writing these words in London last month, it occurred to me that my fountain pen was an admirable example of what I have been describing. It is a pen of American design, assembled in Australia from parts some of which were made there and some shipped from the United States. But being "Australian made," it can sell in England and Western Europe far more freely than if it were imported wholly from America.)

Before any American manufacturer goes ahead and invests capital in a branch factory in the Eastern Hemisphere, he needs to know whether or not this Two-World system is going to continue. For if we are going back to One World, he had better concentrate his production at home. And if the present convertibility of currencies within the Eastern Hemisphere is not going to last, if the Sterling Area or the European Payments Union is going to break down, then equally his factory in Scotland is going to be a bad investment, for instead of supplying half the world, it may finish up by supplying only one or two countries.

It is, therefore, a matter of some importance to a great many people to know what the outlook is. One World? Or Two Worlds? Or Twenty Worlds?

The official policy of the chief governments ever since the war is that One World — in the sense in which I am using it — can and will be reconstructed. The great financial and economic schemes of the immediate post-war years — the Bretton Woods Agreements, the Havana Charter, the Gatt negotiations and a score or more of minor documents — were all specifically based upon that assumption. Nor was this entirely an American philosophy. It is true that it received its main impetus from Washington, and particularly from the traditions that were built in the State Department by Cordell Hull, by Mr. Will Clayton and by others. This American enthusiasm was no doubt, in the circumstances of the post-war years, very compelling on other governments — you don't unnecessarily question Santa Claus's philosophy. But that is not the whole of the story. There was, for example, a genuine belief among the leading British economists that One Financial World could be rebuilt, and the very last words that John Maynard Keynes wrote for publication were an expression of that faith. When the Keynesians and the bankers agreed, it was difficult to disagree.

Nevertheless, I have always been a heretic. I began to form the view before the war that there was an obstruction in the world's exchange markets of a kind and size wholly different from anything that had been previously known. This new factor was a chronic tendency towards a shortage of dollars, and I felt honoured to observe that when Professor Charles Kindleberger of the Massachusetts Institute of Technology published his book entitled "The Dollar Shortage" he found the earliest expression of the idea of a permanent and organic shortage of dollars in an article that I wrote as long ago as September 1937. So you will see that I am a veteran in heresy. And, as is I believe the case with all heretics, the more time passes the more convinced do I become that I am right. I have at least had the gratification of seeing a large number of economists come over to my side, or at the least fall silent on their own. So I am encouraged to be dogmatic, and I will give you a confident prediction. In currency matters, we shall continue to have Two Worlds, as we do now. Neither more nor less. On the one hand, it will not prove possible to dismantle the controls and defences that separate the Dollar Area from the Eastern Hemisphere. And on the other hand, the very substantial degree of freedom of payments that now exists within the Eastern Hemisphere can be expected to continue.

It is, I think, important to bring out what this prediction implies. A government does not impose restrictions upon its citizens' freedom to dispose of their money as they will out of sheer wickedness or devilment. It restricts the purchase of foreign currencies only if the supply of foreign currencies in exchange for its own, relative to the demand for them, is inadequate. In other words, the need for exchange restrictions only arises when the balance of payments has become an imbalance of payments. It follows that restrictions on payments can be avoided, and convertibility can be maintained, only if balances of payments do not get out of kilter. And that in turn implies that adjustments can and will be made to restore an equilibrium that is threatened with disturbance and that the reserves of various kinds will be sufficient to meet any deficit while equilibrium is being re-established.

When, therefore, I assert that convertibility will be maintained within the Eastern Hemisphere, but not between the Eastern Hemisphere and the Dollar Area, I am in fact asserting that the necessary adjustments will be made as between the different countries of the Sterling Area and the European Payments Union, but that the similar adjustments between the Eastern Hemisphere as a whole and the Dollar Area as a whole will not be made. As between the Eastern Hemisphere countries, it will prove possible to keep them roughly in step with each other and to maintain a rough equilibrium in their balances of payments, at least so far as current transactions are concerned, while still leaving individual traders free to pursue their business without having to seek official permission. But as between the one area as a whole and the other area as a whole, it will continue to be true that the only way to bring the two sides of the ledger into balance will be by the brute force of control and restriction.

This is the thesis that I must sustain. The argument is

too large to be fitted in at the end of this lecture, and I must defer it until tomorrow. But perhaps there is still time today to say something, by way of introduction, about the general problem of adjustment in international payments.

When a country's balance of payments gets out of equilibrium — that is, when it finds itself making more payments to foreigners than it is receiving from them (or, of course, *vice versa*, though an excess of credits is, in the nature of things, much less disturbing) — the first brunt falls on the reserves. The country finds its balances in foreign banks running down, and it has to settle its debts in gold or in dollars. If the situation is temporary — a seasonal strain, perhaps, or a passing political scare — it will reverse itself and the reserves will fill up again. But if the cause of the disequilibrium is not temporary, the country will soon have to take steps to correct it before all its reserves are gone — and correction can only mean either an increase in in-payments or a reduction in out-payments or both.

In the classical theory of international trade, there are two main methods of adjustment. The first is a change in the rate of exchange between the country's currency and all other currencies — in other words a devaluation or depreciation. Though this has come to be regarded as the last recourse, it was not so historically. Quite on the contrary, the stability of exchange rates was very largely a nineteenth-century invention. Throughout most of currency history, a change in the exchange rate has been the most usual method of securing equilibrium. A rate of exchange is, after all, only a price, and if the supply of a currency comes to exceed the demand for it, the most natural method of adjustment is to alter the price.

[36]

If this course was not taken, then the other classical method of adjustment was by changes in internal price levels. The loss of gold by the debtor country would, in gold standard days, induce a restriction of credit and a lowering of prices in that country, or at least a stalemate on the domestic market, a reduced rate of imports and a greater anxiety to export. Simultaneously, an inflow of gold in the creditor countries would lead to an inflation of domestic demand, a greater market for imports and some slackening in exports. This, in theory, was the way the gold standard worked, and if you believe that it is wholly imaginary, you should read Professor Jacob Viner's famous study of Canada in the first decade and a half of the present century, published in the Harvard Economic Studies, which shows the theory working out in practice.

That, however, was before both the world wars, back in that blissful era when economies were stable and when governments were wholly innocent of any economic policies other than a protective tariff or two. In the present day, when there is so infinitely more to adjust, governments put very great obstacles in the way of both the classical forms of adjustment. Changes in rates of exchange are considered almost immoral. This is, of course, because they are also unpopular with the democratic electorates. On the Continent of Europe, they arouse memories of the wild currency inflations of the 1920s and 1940s, and a small alteration of a rate of exchange, which may be no more than a recognition of an established state of affairs, will be taken as the signal for a massive flight of liquid capital. In Great Britain, where half the food supply and more than half of the raw materials used in industry, are imported, there is the further complication

[37]

that a fall in the pound sterling causes an immediate rise in the domestic cost of living, with inevitable repercussions on labour relations and the level of wages. For all these reasons, an adjustment in the rate of exchange, though it may be designed to cure an existing disequilibrium between in-payments and exports, tends to set up internal inflationary tendencies which, feeding on themselves, may before long create a new disequilibrium of precisely the kind it was designed to cure. Governments, therefore, without entirely ruling it out, have come to regard it as the weapon of last resort, to be used only if all else fails.

The resistance to the second classical method of adjustment is even stiffer. Let me recall to your minds the fact that, under the gold-standard system, a country that had got into a debtor situation, restricted its credit and imposed on itself enough deflation to get its costs down and make itself once more competitive. Shades of full employment! There is hardly a politician alive in any country today who would stand up in public and advocate the deliberate courting of unemployment simply in order to get level with foreigners, who (as everyone knows) always cheat anyhow and are ready to take all manner of unfair advantages, such as working harder or being more efficient. It is true that several countries have recently been experimenting with tighter and dearer credit, but the chief avowed motive in every case, so far as I know, has been to limit or prevent purely domestic inflation. Moreover, the results, though real, have in many countries been rather disappointingly ineffective. It would appear that in a modern planned and unionised economy there is a great deal of "stickiness" which makes industrial costs slow to respond to monetary controls. Credit

[38]

policy may perhaps still be potent enough to put brakes
upon a rising tendency in wages and profits, and possibly
even to bring it to a halt. This may, indeed, be useful to
a country that is in difficulties with its balance of payments, for even a halt to a rise in costs will help if they go
on rising in other countries. But it is almost inconceiv-
able in most, if not quite in all, democratic countries that
a policy of deliberate disinflation would ever be pressed
so far as to bring about an actual *reduction* in wage rates
or wage costs. This second classical method of securing
equilibrium may therefore still be of some value in making small adjustments and in removing small discrepancies. But no more than that.

The position in the present world, as I see it, is therefore that the normal processes of adjustment, by which
disequilibria in international payments are removed,
have become so clogged and obstructed that they have
much less than their classical potency. The thesis I have
to establish is that while they will nevertheless suffice to
maintain an adequate equilibrium within the Eastern
Hemisphere, they will *not* be enough to restore the balance and to close the gap, in freedom, between the Eastern Hemisphere and the Dollar Area. It is from that
point that I shall begin my last lecture tomorrow.

III

The Scarce Dollar

IN MY SECOND LECTURE, I sketched the main outline of the Two-World system that has developed since the war in matters of international trade and payments. To call it a Two-World system is, in some ways, a misnomer. There is the third world beyond the Iron Curtain. Moreover, even on our side of the great dividing line there are many individual countries, such as Spain, and even whole areas, such as Southern Latin America, that do not fit easily into any classification. Nevertheless, it remains true that by far the greater part of the free trading world falls into one or other of two large groupings, on the one hand the Dollar Area of North America and the independent Caribbean countries, on the other hand, virtually the whole of Western Europe, Africa, Southern Asia and Australasia (which I have been briefly referring to as the Eastern Hemisphere). Within the Eastern Hemisphere, thanks to the institutions of the Sterling Area and the European Payments Union, there is very substantial freedom of payments for all current trading transactions — within the Sterling Area for capital transactions too. But between any country in the Eastern Hemisphere and the Dollar Area, payments even for current trade are subject to considerable and detailed control. It is this state of affairs that I refer to as a Two-World situation.

Furthermore, I advanced the thesis that this state of affairs would continue — that the free trading world would not, on the one hand, relapse into the chaos of a score or two of separate national payments areas which existed in the period immediately after the war, nor, on the other hand, would control be relaxed from the relations between the Eastern Hemisphere and the Dollar Area. I pointed out that to make this prognostication was, in fact, to prophesy that the countries of the Eastern Hemisphere would be both willing and able to make enough adjustments to enable them to keep roughly in step with each other — or alternatively that the divergences would be no more than could be covered by the available reserves — but that as between the Eastern Hemisphere and the Dollar Area, the adjustments necessary to permit a free and uncontrolled balance of payments would not be made. This is my thesis, and in this third and final lecture I must try to sustain it.

I said something also, in my concluding paragraphs yesterday, about the general question of adjustment. There are two broad ways in which, when a nation's balance of payments is threatening to get out of equilibrium, it can be brought back into balance without the imposition of restrictions upon the freedom of business to buy and sell as it will. One is by changes in the rate of exchange — by alterations in the price of one currency in terms of the others. The other is by internal changes in prices and credit conditions, which make one country a better importer's market than another or which place differential premiums on exporting. All this is familiar from the theory of international trade. But in the present day both these classical methods of adjustment are so obstructed by the economic policy of governments that their

[41]

efficacy is much reduced. Moreover, this has happened at a time when the magnitude of the discrepancies to be coped with has greatly increased. Whether or not the classical system ever worked in the way expounded by the textbooks, it is clear that manifold obstacles stand in its way today.

Within the Eastern Hemisphere, however, and as between the countries that compose it, there is some reason to believe that the discrepancies that are likely to arise either are small or at least are no greater than can be carried by the reserves. The European countries are, most of them, mature industrial nations, importing raw materials and tropical produce and exporting manufactures. To a very remarkable extent, they live by taking in each other's washing. The interconnections between them are so close and sensitive that a change in the conjuncture of one tends to be reflected immediately in the others. They cannot get badly out of step with each other, for reasons not of the financial exchanges, but of close industrial interconnections. By the same token, if any disequilibrium does begin to emerge, it can usually be covered by relatively small shifts in credit policy or in prices.

With the non-European members of the Sterling Area, the case is, of course, different. Though many of these countries — Australia, for example, — have developed their industries considerably in recent decades, they are still dependent for their international earnings on exports of primary products, agricultural and mineral. This is the sort of economy that is subject to wide swings between riches and poverty. So far from resembling the relations of the European countries with one another, which I have just been describing, when one of these primary producing economies is caught up in one of its swings, whether it be up or down, there is very little that anyone can do about it. But in these cases there is the long tradition of dependence on the London money market, which absorbs in good years the greater part of the mounting credits, and which has always been willing — within limits, but they are very wide limits — to "carry" a Sterling Area country that is in a cycle of deficit. Western Europe (including the United Kingdom) and the non-European members of the Sterling Area are, to quite a large extent, complementary to each other. When one is in surplus the other is in deficit; and if these balances had all to be currently settled in gold or dollars, one or the other would always be in trouble. But the internal settlement and credit-extending mechanisms of the Sterling Area and the European Payments Union deal with the problem with a fair measure of success — not indeed sufficient to solve the problem of a chronic debtor such as France has become, but enough to deal with all normal exigencies.

For these reasons, it is permissible to hope — though I acknowledge that it requires some optimism — that, within what I have described as the Eastern Hemisphere, the mechanisms of adjustment by means of fiscal and credit policy will be sufficient to bring divergent balances of payments back into equilibrium before the reserves are exhausted, and that, in consequence, the present substantial degree of freedom of trade and payments within the Eastern Hemisphere will at least be maintained. In deed, the air is full, as you know, of plans for extending it — for creating a Common Market between six of the European countries and a Free Trade Area — at least in manufactures — between those six and another six, of which the United Kingdom is one. The documents embodying these plans all make formal reservation of the rights of any country to withdraw if it finds itself in balance-of-payments trouble.   But I think it is obvious that if they thought this was at all likely, or more than an insurance against an unlikely emergency, they would not be willing to contemplate entering into the engagements that are now under discussion.   Rightly or wrongly, it is the opinion of the competent authorities that the adjustment mechanisms will work sufficiently well to avoid any necessity to balance the books by the *force majeure* of controls, licences and prohibitions.   At the most, there should not be in the Eastern Hemisphere any discrepancies that relatively small movements in exchange rates will not suffice to correct.

If this is the outlook within the Eastern Hemisphere, why not also between Hemispheres?   Why cannot the same optimism be felt about the gradual removal of controls from the trade between the Eastern Hemisphere and the Dollar Area, until it too can be left to the free decisions of individual traders, subject only to such influence as may be exerted by credit policy, by interest rates, by the tightness or availability of money or — in the last resort — by small variations in the rates of exchange?   If optimism is in order in the one case, why not in the other?

The brief answer, in my opinion, is that the maladjustments are far too large for the normal mechanisms to cope with.   There are two sides to the medal.   The reasons for optimism in the Eastern Hemisphere are, firstly, that the discrepancies to be apprehended are relatively small, and, secondly, either that the normal adjusting mechanisms can be expected to be effective or else that the available reserves are sufficient.   Neither is true of trade between the dollar and non-dollar worlds.   The gap to be bridged

[44]

is very wide. The adjusting mechanisms are likely to be relatively ineffective. And the reserves available to the potential debtors are small relatively to the total of transactions passing.

All these things are reflections of the enormous relative economic strength of the United States — a position of relative strength without any parallel in economic history. Certainly the only possible parallel would be with the economic and financial supremacy of Great Britain in the middle years of the nineteenth century. Even there, though it is difficult to compare two such different situations, it would be my judgment that Britain was never as strong relatively to the rest of the world as the United States is now — her customers were never as dependent on her, nor was she so nearly independent of them, as contemporary America is. It is an interesting speculation whether this state of affairs would have come about without the two world wars. In my opinion, it would to some degree, as it rests on factors that are inherent in natural resources and the structure of the different national economies. But it might have happened much more gradually and perhaps to a lesser extent. It was certainly accelerated, and perhaps exaggerated, by the two wars. In both of them the fighting took place, not in America, but in and around the other major economic powers. Quite naturally, therefore, America's industrial potential was rapidly developed under the enormous pressures of these two wars, while her competitors' economies were being distorted, diverted and in some cases destroyed. I hope you will acquit me of any attempt to pass any moral judgments, which is not in the least my intention. The fact is that the two world wars, and especially the second, took a course which left the American national economy, when

[45]

the fighting ended, more able, and the other countries' economies less able, to earn a normal peacetime living than they had been. Moreover, the evolutions between the various stages of Debtor and Creditor status that I described in my first lecture, instead of being gradual and leaving time for the necessary economic and psychological adjustments, were crowded into a few years.

Whatever the causes, the phenomenon is there — and a remarkable phenomenon it is. The world has an urgent and swelling demand for American products. In some cases, this is because the economies of mass production for the enormous domestic market enable the American product to be cheaper and better than its rivals. The archetype of this is the American automobile. But in other cases — and I think this is the more significant example — it is because American technology is in advance of that of other countries. In industry after industry, it is not simply that the American machine is better or cheaper, it is the only one obtainable that will do the job. Let me give you two widely separated examples, neither of them a new industry. In printing, particularly (but not exclusively) the high-speed printing of mass media, there are American machines that can do what no other country's machines can do. A printer who wants to be up to date in his technology must buy American machines whatever they cost. Secondly, in the heavier sorts of highway construction, you either use American machinery or your highways take many times as long to get built. I have taken two examples that have fallen under my notice; I have no doubt at all that they could be multiplied twenty or fifty times. The size of the internal market in the United States, the long start that America has acquired in the application of capital to industrial ends, the enormous volume of research, the supply of capital available, the pressure for speed in technological advance that is built up by the intensely competitive atmosphere of American industry — all these things make it very difficult for other countries to keep up, and hopeless for them to catch up. Moreover, it is hard to see how this state of affairs can alter, so long as the present era of rapid technological advance and heavy capital investment continues unabated.

On the other side of the fence, the demand of the United States for the products of the Eastern Hemisphere is neither very elastic nor very urgent. When I say that it is not very elastic, I should perhaps say "not very elastic on the down side." Of very few Eastern Hemisphere products that sell in the American market can it be said that the American demand for them would increase substantially if they were cheaper. If they are manufactures, they sell chiefly on design, fashion or novelty, not price. If they are raw materials, the quantities bought depend on the activity of American industry. Reductions in price will not lead to more being sold; increases in price, on the other hand, will in a significant number of cases lead to substitutions, as of synthetic for natural rubber or of domestic aluminum for imported copper. I can see on your lips the unspoken question "But what of the Paley Report, with its story of a rapidly growing U.S. dependence on imports of raw materials of all kinds?" I have not forgotten the Paley Report. Though for the moment I have been speaking of the United States, my argument really relates to the Dollar Area, which extends from Baffin Land to the jungles of the Orinoco. If you analyse the figures of the Paley Report with care, you will see that, in the great majority of cases, the increased imports of raw materials on which the United States will depend will

[47]

come either from Canada or from the Caribbean area.
The Paley Report is a charter of economic hope for your
dollar-using neighbours. There is relatively little in it
for the Eastern Hemisphere. Nor is oil nearly as big an
exception to what I am saying as might appear at first
sight. It is true that Europe, when the Suez Canal is
open, does not now need to buy nearly as much petro-
leum from the Dollar Area as formerly. But what is
called the "dollar content" of the Middle Eastern oil —
that is, the proportion of the total cost that has to be met,
directly or indirectly, in dollars — is still quite considerable.

The effect of all this is, as I have said already, to create
a situation without any precedent, or even an approach
to a precedent, in economic history. It is so for two quite
separate reasons. First, the relation of the elasticities of
demand must be almost unique. It is difficult to believe
that there can ever have been another case of a country
where the demand of the rest of the world for its products
was so urgent, and its demand for the products of the rest
of the world so indifferent — where rises in price would
choke off so few sales on the one side and falls in price
stimulate so few purchases on the other — as is the case
with the United States today. Secondly, there is the size
of the trade involved. If it were a small country that was
in such a strong position — a Switzerland, say, or a Belgium — it could perhaps pile up its assets without ex-
hausting the reserves of the rest of the world. But the
United States is the world's largest trading nation. I made
a rough estimate some years ago that if there were no dis-
criminating controls in the rest of the world on American
goods — if, that is to say, the citizen of every country in
the world were as free to buy from the United States as

[48]

he is to buy from other foreign countries — then the favourable balance of payments on account of current transactions would be in excess of $10 billion a year and might be much more. And this is without allowing for the stream of capital that would seek to invest itself in this country if it were allowed to do so. The gold and dollar reserves of the rest of the world are clearly quite inadequate to cope with a drain of that magnitude. Nor, generous though the American people have been in grants of economic aid, is it practical politics to think of aid payments on anything like that scale. It follows that, so long as this state of affairs continues, freedom of trade and payments between the Eastern Hemisphere and the Dollar Area is an impossibility. The Eastern Hemisphere, taken as a whole, will have to be most watchful, through all manner of licencing devices, to see that it does not allow its citizens to spend more dollars than come into the till.

"So long as this state of affairs continues." But cannot anything be done to bring it to an end? Is it not possible for the non-dollar world to adjust itself to this great strength of the dollar? Is the world trading system so rigid that the two sides of the account could not be brought into balance by the normal mechanisms of the price system, stimulated by the enterprise of merchants and industrialists? I am not taking the position that the adjustment will never be made. Undoubtedly it will, at some time and by some means. Nothing in this world is permanent and even the greatest economic leads can in time be overtaken, as we in England have the best reason to know. But I do say that — short of some cataclysm, such as another world war which, for a change, is fought in America and not in Europe — short of something quite unpredictable, adjustment is going to take a very long time.

[49]

For how would it proceed? Let me revert to the two classical mechanisms. The first is changes in the rate of exchange between the dollar — or perhaps I should say the dollars — and the Eastern Hemisphere currencies. I am far from saying that there is no conceivable rate of exchange between the dollar and the pound sterling (taking the pound to typify the Eastern Hemisphere currencies) that would bring their balances of payments into an uncontrolled equilibrium. If dollars are made, to the rest of the world, dearer and dearer and dearer, a point is presumably reached some time when American goods are so fantastically expensive in terms of other countries' currencies that the demand for them is choked off. Similarly, if European goods are made dirt cheap for Americans to buy, presumably the sales of them do go up. What I am asserting is that the rate of exchange would have to move a very long way before it was sufficient by itself to balance the books. Suppose, for example, that the pound sterling falls from $2.80 to $1.40. Sales of American goods in the Sterling Area would certainly be reduced. But would they be halved? When you remember that for years they have been controlled down to the bare essentials, I very much doubt it. If British goods were halved in price in America, more would be sold. But twice as many? Again, I doubt it — yet if the increase were less than 100%, the result would be that Britain was earning even fewer dollars by her exports than now. Thus even as a simple academic exercise in relative elasticities, I think the change in price would have to be very large indeed before the uncontrolled supply and demand curves for pounds in exchange for dollars could be made to coincide — if, indeed, there is any such price.

As a practical matter, solution by exchange rate is even

[50]

more doubtful than it is in theory. For exchange rates are controlled by governments, and neither the British nor the American government would for an instant contemplate a change as large as would be necessary. Furthermore, even if equilibrium were by this means restored for an instant of time, it would not last a month, because of the inflationary tendencies that it would set up within the devaluating countries. And, finally, if all these problems could be solved in respect of current transactions, it would still not be possible to remove exchange control because of the enormous pressure that a large devaluation would set up for the flight of capital from the Eastern Hemisphere to the United States.

The second classical method of adjustment is by divergent tendencies of internal costs and prices in the two areas. Maynard Keynes, in the last months of his life, attached his hopes to the belief that the inflation of costs in the United States would rapidly restore equilibrium. But clearly he has been proved wrong. Rapid rises in American wage levels there have certainly been. But the rise in the productivity of labour has been almost as rapid, with the result that, on the whole, the level of manufacturing costs in the United States, relatively to the level in other countries, has been falling rather than rising. Furthermore, suppose this tendency could be reversed, and Eastern Hemisphere goods could be made progressively cheaper than American, how much effect would there be on the balance of trade? Some, certainly; but again, I think relatively little. For there are so many American goods that the world wants whatever they cost. And there are so many American imports of which the quantity bought is not likely to increase as the price goes down.

I stay, therefore, by my conclusion — that this par-

[51]

ticular disequilibrium, uniquely in economic history, is so large in volume and so unresponsive to adjustment in its nature, that it is likely to remain with us for a very long time.

You will perhaps have noticed that I have argued my case without once mentioning those political manifestations that are usually given the greatest prominence in discussions of the subject — the United States tariff, the "Buy American" Act and the like. The omission was deliberate. The essence of my argument is that the world dollar shortage is an organic thing, emerging out of the facts of economic life among the nations, not out of the political acts of any legislature. Dollars are short because America is strong, not because Congress is misguided. Even were every shred and scrap of American protection to be removed tomorrow, even if the tariff were totally repealed, the problem would still remain. That having been said, however, I do think it is fair to add that the tariff and the other obstructions to imports into the United States have acquired a symbolic importance far greater than their real effect. They discourage the non-American nations from making even such efforts as they could to narrow the gap. And in this respect it is not so much the height of the tariff itself that does harm as the widespread belief in other countries that if they do succeed in selling in the American market over the tariff wall, it will be raised against them. There are, it is true, not many examples of that actually being done; but every one reverberates round the trading world.

As I said yesterday, it is now nearly twenty years since I first formed the view that the shortage of dollars, the chronic tendency to a favourable balance of payments for the United States, was a unique phenomenon and one

[52]

that would prove most stubborn to remove. I don't know that I have ever needed the passage of time to convince me that any of my opinions was well-founded. But certainly time has been my ally in this instance. Before I finally nail down the dogma, however, let me take a look at some of the things that still might upset it.

First, let me make it clear that, in predicting a continuing shortage of dollars for the Eastern Hemisphere, I am not prophesying that it will be so every day, or every month, or even every year. I am sure there will be times when, through some coincidence of factors, there will seem to be more dollars on offer than are bid for. There was such a flurry last year (though of a very special kind), and I have no doubt there will be others. I am speaking of the average of years, of the secular tendency.

Secondly, there is the possibility that dollar aid of one sort or another will be forthcoming in such volume as to close the gap. No one ought to discuss this subject in public — certainly no Englishman — without paying his tribute of praise and gratitude to the willingness of the American people and government to help their neighbours in such volume and over so many years. We can say of it, as Sir Winston Churchill said of lend-lease, that it is the most unsordid act of which history has record. I wish I could believe that my own people would have done as much if the roles had been reversed.

Nevertheless, I do not believe that economic aid can be relied upon to solve the problem of the dollar gap. I have two reasons. One is a matter of definition. The problem of the gap will not be solved, to my way of thinking, until the books are balanced by ordinary trade and financial transactions, freely initiated by free citizens, without the necessity for controls and prohibitions on the one hand or

[53]

for artificial governmental stimulants on the other. American economic aid, like British exchange control, is not a means for bringing the two legs of the balance of payments into agreement with each other, so much as a crutch that has to be provided because the patient limps.

Secondly, there is the matter of size. There is a large programme of economic aid in existence today, and though it certainly helps, it equally certainly does not close the gap, as witness the continuance of exchange controls. Only if you can imagine the total of economic aid being twice or three times what it is now, and continuing at that level indefinitely, can it be thought of as providing enough dollars to meet the demand for them.

What I would accept as a natural solution would be a large outflow of freely offered capital, going out from the Dollar Area to the undeveloped countries of the Eastern Hemisphere. Here we come back to the subject with which my first lecture was concerned — the different shapes of the balances of payments of different nations at different stages of their growth. Heaven knows there is plenty of scope in the world for further development, and though capital alone will not do it, it cannot be done without capital. On the one side we have a great country so rich that the difficulty is to know what it can do with its surplus international earnings. On the other side we have enormous areas of the world which have only recently woken up to the fact that they are poor and could be rich. Is there not here an almost infinite field for the fruitful investment of dollars?

In theory, yes. In practice, I am more doubtful. Where the process of international investment works best is where both ends of the process, the lender in the mature country and the borrower in the undeveloped country, understand each other and are trying to do the same thing. That is why it works so well between the United States and Canada, where the lender and the borrower speak the same language in the metaphorical as well as the literal sense. That is why it worked so well in the last century between Great Britain and the United States. The same conditions exist where the borrowing country is undeveloped in the social and political sense as well as the economic, and will let the overseas capitalist come in and supervise the investment of his money. That is the way the pampas of Argentina were opened up by British money. That is the way (broadly speaking) in which the deserts of the Middle East are being developed, largely by American money. But the supply of undeveloped open spaces is limited, and where the process of investment takes the form of foreign capital pushing its way into highly organised and complex societies, then the obstacles and the obstructions are manifold. They have been admirably described recently in Mr. Maurice Zinkin's book "Development for Free Asia" — a book which I would like to commend to you so highly as being at once the most sensible and the most readable treatment of its subject that has come my way, that I will ask you to excuse a somewhat extended quotation from it. "The price of development" says Mr. Zinkin

> is high; a society which wishes to develop must be prepared to put development in the very forefront of its priorities, to want development harder than it wants anything else. The mechanics of development are difficult and very liable to go wrong; unless a country wants to increase its income very badly indeed, it will flinch at the difficulties; every time something goes wrong it will find solace in other, and older, satisfactions. One need not

[55]

go so far as the Communists, with whom development takes precedence of the Ten Commandments. But the people of a country which wishes to develop must at least be willing to replace the generosity of ceremony and festival by skimping thrift, to exchange the pleasure of lying on a cot in the shade for back-breaking work, to buy savings bonds and share certificates instead of adorning their wives. Most difficult of all for many societies, contract must replace status, a measure of planning *laisser-faire*. The rich, the educated, the well-born must accept equality with the poor, the illiterate and those without grandfathers. All must reconcile themselves to the disappearance of the easy freedom of the law-and-order State; one cannot have a welfare State without the pettifogging interference of minor officials.

. . . . .

In underdeveloped societies this may well mean turning society upside down. They are poor to a very considerable extent precisely because their values have not emphasised becoming rich. The areas, like the Amazon valley, which are poor by nature are the exception; Indonesia is not naturally poorer than Holland. Asia's difficulty is much more that its values give a low place to economics and change and making money, a high place to stability, saintliness and power. If it is more important to be in the winning snakeboat team at the Annual Regatta than to grow more rice to the acre, better regarded to be a Sub-Inspector of Police than the largest of shopkeepers, and a quicker way to Heaven to become a hermit than to give away one's self-made millions, then clearly the economic operation of society will be left to its least desirable or least dynamic members; and the undesirable and the backward can hardly be expected to do much developing.

. . . . .

[56]

So high a price will not be accepted unless development becomes the central point of the people's ambitions as well as of State policy. Those who would rather go to the cinema than save the price of the seat, rather earn less in the place they know than be uncomfortable somewhere else, rather work hard at their hobbies than put something extra into their daily routine may daydream about development; they cannot really want it.

. . . . .

. . . Those who want to be rich so that they can become powerful or so that their intelligentsia may be respected amongst the educated of the rest of the world find it difficult to settle down to the long haul of sacrifice and work and acceptance of unpleasant change that development demands. They are too easily diverted. They buy arms instead of building dams; their best brains become professors of literature instead of technologists; they choose showy schemes rather than profitable ones; their rich men, like Arab oil-kings, buy Cadillacs instead of irrigating their land.[1]

It is not Mr. Zinkin's conclusion, nor is it the conclusion that I would suggest to you, that there is no scope at all for the investment of capital in the development of the poor countries of the world. Far from it. But I do suggest that the amount that can be usefully so invested, and that is not being invested already, is limited. A study which was recently published by the Special Congressional Committee To Study the Foreign Aid Program and which had been prepared for them by The Center for International Studies of the Massachusetts Institute of Technology made an attempt to estimate what might perhaps be accomplished under this head. They found that

[1] Maurice Zinkin, *Development for Free Asia* (London, Chatto and Windus; Fair Lawn, New Jersey, Essential Books, 1956), pp. 4, 5, 6.

[57]

it depended on what they called the "absorptive capacity"
of the undeveloped countries.

Absorptive capacity is limited by a wide range of factors,
some fairly easily measurable, others intangible and elu-
sive. A project may not be feasible because the raw materials it requires are not available; because there is in-
sufficient power to operate it or inadequate transport
facilities to bring in inputs and take away outputs; because too few people in the country have the required
skills to make up the work force or the necessary train-
ing, experience, and drive to manage the enterprise; and
so on. Or a sufficient market may not yet have developed within the country for the product of a proposed
enterprise to justify its construction. Many projects are
complementary to each other and should be undertaken
simultaneously. But if too many projects are undertaken at once there may be bottlenecks of resources
which cannot be imported and the price of which will
rise enough to threaten the economy with a general inflation. The intangibles include such things as the development consciousness of the people, the imagination
and courage with which they pursue new opportunities
and ideas, their willingness to take long-term risks, and
the adaptability of the labor force to new technical tasks.

The M.I.T. group came to the conclusion that 2\frac{1}{2}$ to
3\frac{1}{2}$ billion per year, additional to what is being done al-
ready, would probably cover everything that could in fact
usefully be done. So far as my own judgment goes, I
would endorse that range of figures. Indeed, as a measure
of the correction that could be brought to the balance of
payments of the United States by expansion of the capital
account it is an overstatement, for three reasons. First,
this is intended to represent the total of development
loans, from all sources. For political reasons if for no oth-

ers, it is important that the United States should not be the sole source of development capital. Indeed, Congress will rightly insist that others should contribute according to their means. Secondly, the briefest glance at the tables of figures which accompanied my first lecture will show that a great deal of the international lending and borrowing that has been going on since the war has not been development capital so much as emergency reserve money. We must hope and believe that the necessity for this is passing. This will be a good thing to the extent that it reflects the rehabilitation of dislocated economies like the French and the Argentine. But the disappearance of loans of this character will be a factor tending to reduce the export of capital from the United States. Thirdly, if we are considering the possibility of international capital movements developing to such an extent as to cover the dollar gap and facilitate the removal of control from the exchanges, we must remember that the attractions of the United States itself as a field of investment are very great and, with more freedom to do so, there would be much more foreign money coming into Wall Street.

For all these reasons, though I will join with anyone in applauding the development of international investment, I cannot see it, in our lifetime, closing the dollar gap, or bringing on to the world's exchange markets a flow of dollars large enough to meet the demand for dollars that would exist if the citizenry of the world were not restrained by their respective laws from demanding them. By various devices — of which the continued generous willingness of the United States to provide economic aid in one form or another is one — a complete breakdown of the exchanges will be avoided. But it will not ever be possible, in our lifetime, for the countries of the Eastern

Hemisphere wholly to remove their controls on the purchase of dollars and therefore their discrimination against American goods.

The Two-World system, in short, will continue. That is a pity, for so one must think if one believes in the maximum possible degree of economic freedom and in the greatest possible division of labour. But I would like to suggest to you that it is not the unmitigated disaster that was predicted by the enthusiasts for "One World" in the years immediately after the war. On the economic plane, the fact that it is Two Worlds, and not twenty or eighty, means that there is still plenty of scope for the division of labour and for the healthy astringent force of competition. Within the Eastern Hemisphere, and particularly in Western Europe, the wind is blowing quite strongly for competition. It is regrettable that trade cannot be what I may perhaps call omnilateral. But it is, and increasingly will be, multilateral, and that is perhaps what matters most.

Politically, the fear used to be expressed that the free world cannot have political unity if it is economically divided. But we have enough experience now to know that it just is not so. The degree of political unity that the free world has achieved has varied, in the post-war decade, from time to time. I cannot recall a single instance in which it has been hindered by the persistence of a payments barrier between the two hemispheres. Official American opinion which, under the impulsion of Mr. Cordell Hull, Mr. Will Clayton and others, started the decade passionately resentful of anything that seemed to smack of discrimination against American exports, has learned to adjust itself to this particular form of discrimination. After all, Europeans cannot be expected to spend

[60]

more dollars than they have and, having exhausted their dollars, it is really not reasonable to object to their using the pounds and francs and lire they do have. Why should I be prevented from spending my vacation at Monte Carlo simply because I do not have the dollars to go to Miami?

We are already learning to live with our Two-World system. No one has adapted himself to it more quickly, or in a more realistic spirit, than the American business-man. It creates complications for him in his export trade, but what are complications but challenges to inge-nuity and enterprise? Such, I am sure, is the spirit that animates the great institution in whose halls I have been privileged to lay these reflections before you.

TABLES

TABLE 1

TYPES OF BALANCES OF PAYMENTS

	Balance of Trade Visible and Invisible + = Favorable − = Unfavorable	Interest and Dividends + = Net Receipt − = Net Payment	Capital + = Borrowing (or Accepting Repayment) − = Lending (or Repaying)
	In all three columns, + signifies a net in-payment, − signifies a net out-payment; two symbols signify a larger payment than one.		
Class A — Immature Debtor-Borrowers	−	−	+
Class B — Mature Debtor-Borrowers	+	− −	+
Class C — Debtor-Lenders and Debtor-Repayers	+ +	−	−
Class D — Immature Credit or Lenders	+	+	−
Class E — Mature Creditor-Lenders	−	+ +	−
Class F — Creditor-Borrowers	− −	+	+

[64]

TABLE 2

BALANCES OF PAYMENTS, 1937

The figures are in millions of U.S. dollars of the pre-1933 gold parity. They refer in the main to the year 1937. A *plus* sign signifies a net *in-payment* of funds and therefore a net *outward* movement of merchandise, services or gold; a *minus* sign signifies a net *out-payment* of funds and therefore a net *inward* movement of merchandise, services or gold.

	Balance of Trade, Visible and Invisible	Interest and Dividends	Balance on Income Account	Lending or Borrowing	Gold	Balance on Capital Account
Class A — Immature						
Debtor-Borrowers						
None						
Class B — Mature						
Debtor-Borrowers						
South Africa	+23	−62	−39	+39	(a)	+39
Poland	+10	−20	−10	+24	−14	+10
Australia	+77	−87	−10	−17	+27	+10
Class C — Debtor-						
Lenders and						
Debtor-Repayers						
New Zealand	+22	−21	+1	−4	+3	−1
Czechoslovakia	+19	−11	+8	−7	−1	−8
Finland	+13	−3	+10	−12	+2	−10
India	+85	−72	+13	−75	+62	−13
Denmark	+25	−10	+15	−15	0	−15
Norway	+25	−10	+15	−20	+ 5	−15
Argentina	+151	−90	+61	−61	0	−61
Canada	+251	−142	+109	−109	(a)	−109
Class D — Immature						
Creditor-Lenders						
Sweden	+12	+15	+27	−27	0	−27
United States	+277	+197	+474	+494	−968	−474
Class E — Mature						
Creditor-Lenders						
Netherlands	−40	+52	+12	+230	−242	−12
Class F — Creditor-						
Borrowers						
France	−313	+154	−157	−98	+255	+157
United Kingdom	−787	+613	−174	+405	−231	+174

(a) Canada and South Africa are gold producers; gold is therefore included as merchandise.

Source: "Balances of Payments, 1938" (League of Nations).

TABLE 3

BALANCES OF PAYMENTS, 1949-1951

The figures are in millions of U.S. dollars. They are, in the main, averages of the three years 1949, 1950, and 1951. A *plus* sign signifies a net *in-payment* of funds and therefore a net *outward* movement of merchandise, service or gold; a *minus* sign signifies a net *out-payment* of funds and therefore a net *inward* movement of merchandise, service or gold.

	Balance of Trade, Visible and Invisible	Interest and Dividends	Balance on Income Account	Lending or Borrowing	Gold	Balance on Capital Account
Class A — Immature Debtor-Borrowers						
France (a)	−644	−11	−655	+659	−4	+655
West Germany	−441	−1	−442	+451	−9	+442
Greece	−302	−3	−305	+304	+1	+305
South Africa	−143	−110	−253	+295	−42 (b)	+253
India	−184	−50	−234	+234	0	+234
Italy	−195	−11	−206	+285	−79	+206
Austria	−200	−1	−201	+201	0	+201
Yugoslavia	−160	−3	−163	+160	+3	+163
Brazil	−37	−123	−160	+161	−1	+160
Norway	−99	−11	−110	+110	0	+110
Argentina	−86	−14	−100	+125	−25	+100
Denmark	−62	−12	−74	+74	0	+74
Turkey	−51	−9	−60	+56	+4	+60
Japan	−22	−4	−26	+30	−4	+26
Peru	−5	−14	−19	+28	−9	+19
Iceland (c)	−10	0	−10	+10	0	+10

Class B — Mature Debtor-Borrowers						
Canada (c)	+137	−324	−187	+335	−148 (b)	+187
Chile	+13	−59	−46	+43	+3	+46
Iran	+384	−406	−22	+20	+2	+22
Mexico	+57	−78	−21	+76	−55	+21
Egypt	+15	−34	−19	+60	−41	+19
Iraq	+25	−40	−15	+15	0	+15
Venezuela	+348	−363	−15	+32	−17	+15
Class C — Debtor-Lenders and Debtor-Repayers						
Pakistan	+10	−4	+6	−6	0	−6
Finland	+28	−11	+17	−15	−2	−17
Australia	+150	−121	+29	−25	−4	−29
New Zealand	+53	−19	+34	−27	−7	−34
Class D — Immature Creditor-Lenders						
Sweden	+100	+6	+106	−81	−25	−106
United States (c)	+2,543	+1,710	+4,253	−4,762	+509	−4,253
Class E — Mature Creditor-Lenders						
Belgium-Luxembourg	−6	+10	+4	−4	0	−4
United Kingdom	−328	+378	+50	+162	−212	−50
Class F — Creditor-Borrowers						
Portugal (c) (d)	−53	+5	−48	+60	−12	+48
Netherlands	−186	+52	−134	+169	−35	+134

(a) France and franc area.
(b) Monetary gold only; exports of newly-mined gold included in visible trade.
(c) Excluding all shipments of military goods and services under aid and corresponding grants; monetary aid payments and receipts included under capital.
(d) Portugal and escudo area.
Source: "Balance of Payments Yearbook, Volume 6, 1953-54" (International Monetary Fund).

TABLE 4

BALANCES OF PAYMENTS, 1952-1954

The figures are in millions of U.S. dollars. They are, in the main, averages of the three years 1952, 1953, and 1954. A *plus* sign signifies a net *in-payment* of funds and therefore a net *outward* movement of merchandise, services, or gold; a *minus* sign signifies a net *out-payment* of funds and therefore a net *inward* movement of merchandise, services, or gold.

	Balance of Trade, Visible and Invisible	Interest and Dividends	Balance on Income Account	Lending or Borrowing	Gold	Balance on Capital Account
Class A — Immature Debtor-Borrowers						
Italy	−424	−10	−434	+438	−4	+434
Brazil	−195	−124	−319	+320	−1	+319
Australia	−158	−133	−291	+291	0	+291
France (a)	−154	−23	−177	+152	+25	+177
Turkey	−153	−6	−159	+157	+2	+159
Yugoslavia	−149	−8	−157	+158	−1	+157
South Africa	−1	−142	−143	+188	−45 (b)	+143
Pakistan	−114	−4	−118	+122	−4	+118
Greece	−109	−2	−111	+113	−2	+111
Norway	−97	−9	−106	+106	0	+106
Egypt	−21	−34	−55	+55	0	+55
Peru	−25	−21	−46	+43	+3	+46
India	−27	−15	−42	+42	0	+42
New Zealand	−36	−5	−41	+43	−2	+41
Japan	−16	−23	−39	+37	+2	+39
Argentina	−15	−8	−23	+57	−34	+23
Denmark	−2	−10	−12	+12	0	+12
Iceland	−4	−1	−5	+5	0	+5

Class B — Mature Debtor-Borrowers						
Canada (c)	+78	−273	−195	+273	−78 (b)	+195
Iran	+1	−60	−59	+59	0	+59
Mexico	+24	−76	−52	+3	+49	+52
Chile	+36	−54	−18	+17	+1	+18
Class C — Debtor-Lenders and Debtor-Repayers						
Finland	+28	−11	+17	−2	−15	−17
Iraq	+198	−141	+57	−57	0	−57
Venezuela	+509	−441	+68	−68	0	−68
West Germany	+856	−23	+833	−634	−199	−833
Class D — Immature Creditor-Lenders						
Portugal (d)	0	+3	+3	+52	−55	−3
Austria	+11	+1	+12	−10	−2	−12
Sweden	+12	+15	+27	+11	−38	−27
Belgium-Luxembourg	+36	+16	+52	−4	−48	−52
Switzerland	+158	+96	+244	−223	−21	−244
Netherlands	+250	+66	+316	−155	−161	−316
United Kingdom	+226	+234	+460	−318	−142	−460
Class E — Mature Creditor-Lenders						
United States (c)	−80	+2,817	+2,107	−2,467	+360	−2,107
Class F — Creditor-Borrowers						
None						

(a) France and franc area.
(b) Monetary gold only; exports of newly-mined gold included in visible trade.
(c) Excluding all shipments of military goods and services under aid and corresponding grants; monetary aid payments and receipts included under capital.
(d) Portugal and escudo area.
Source: "Balance of Payments Yearbook, Volume 6, 1953–54" (International Monetary Fund).

[69]

TABLE 5

BALANCE OF PAYMENTS OF THE UNITED STATES, 1954

The figures are in millions of dollars. A *plus* sign denotes a net receipt of funds by the United States and therefore a net *outward* movement of merchandise or services; a *minus* sign denotes a net payment of funds by the United States and therefore a net *inward* movement of merchandise or services.

	Canada	Latin America	Sterling Area	Other OEEC Countries	Other Countries	Total
1. Merchandise Trade	+501	−120	+216	+971	+817	+2,385
2. Services	+ 14	+ 18	−430	−1,284	−688	−2,370
3. Balance of Trade (1 + 2)	+515	−102	−214	−313	+129	+ 15
4. Interest and Dividends	+442	+786	+452	+149	+429	+2,258
5. Total, Current Transactions (3 + 4)	+957	+684	+238	−164	+558	+2,273
6. Donations	+ 2	− 84	−298	−969	−679	−2,028
7. Long-term Lending (−) or Borrowing (+)	−747	−298	− 81	+236	−329	−1,219
8. Total of Above Remaining to Be Settled	+212	+302	−141	−897	−450	− 974

Source: U. S. Department of Commerce.

[70]